______________'S TRAINING DIARY

#TrackLife — Athlete Training Diary: Your Elite Planner (Alternate Fourth Edition)

Copyright © Torema Thompson, 2023. All rights reserved.

ISBN: 978-1-8384368-7-2

First published in the UK by Pura Track Publishing in August 2023.

For business enquiries, email: questions@toremathompson.uk

PERSONAL DETAILS

SEASON: 20____ / 20 ____

Name	
Phone	
Email	
Club	
Event(s)	
Personal Best(s)	
Coach(es)	
Instagram	
Twitter	

In case of emergency please contact:

Name	
Phone	
Email	

MY BIG GOAL THIS SEASON

COMPETITION SCHEDULE

Date	Meeting / Location	Event(s)	Results

KEY SETTINGS

Equipment / Event	Date	Settings / Measurements / Notes
[Example] Blocks	01.08.23	Front (L) – 2 feet / Back (R) – 3 feet (1 up)

TRAINING / ATHLETICS NEEDS

Item	Due By	Details
[Example] Weightlifting shoes	01.10.23	Adidas Adipower weightlifting II shoes - ss22 / Sportsshoes.com £99.99

MONTH:

EVERY RACE IS WON, ONE STEP AT A TIME.

#TrackLife

Monthly Goals

DATE GOALS SET:

LIFESTYLE (E.G. SLEEP, NUTRITION, PUNCTUALITY ETC.)
TECHNICAL / TACTICAL
FAMILY / SOCIAL
PHYSICAL FITNESS / HEALTH
MENTAL / EMOTIONAL / SPIRITUAL
WORK / EDUCATION

Training Overview

WEEKLY TRAINING DIARY

DATE:

TRAINING WEEK NO:

MONDAY
TUESDAY
WEDNESDAY
THURSDAY

WEEKLY TRAINING DIARY

FRIDAY

SATURDAY

SUNDAY

NOTES

WEEKLY TRAINING DIARY

DATE: TRAINING WEEK NO:

MONDAY
TUESDAY
WEDNESDAY
THURSDAY

WEEKLY TRAINING DIARY

FRIDAY

SATURDAY

SUNDAY

NOTES

WEEKLY TRAINING DIARY

DATE: TRAINING WEEK NO:

MONDAY
TUESDAY
WEDNESDAY
THURSDAY

WEEKLY TRAINING DIARY

FRIDAY

SATURDAY

SUNDAY

NOTES

WEEKLY TRAINING DIARY

DATE: TRAINING WEEK NO:

MONDAY
TUESDAY
WEDNESDAY
THURSDAY

WEEKLY TRAINING DIARY

FRIDAY

SATURDAY

SUNDAY

NOTES

WEEKLY TRAINING DIARY

DATE: TRAINING WEEK NO:

MONDAY

TUESDAY

WEDNESDAY

THURSDAY

WEEKLY TRAINING DIARY

FRIDAY

SATURDAY

SUNDAY

NOTES

Monthly Goals Review

REVIEW YOUR GOALS FROM THE PAST MONTH.
DID YOU ACHIEVE THEM? IF YES, WHAT WORKED WELL?
IF NOT, WHAT WILL YOU DO DIFFERENTLY NEXT MONTH?

LIFESTYLE (E.G. SLEEP, NUTRITION, PUNCTUALITY ETC.)
TECHNICAL / TACTICAL
FAMILY / SOCIAL
PHYSICAL FITNESS / HEALTH
MENTAL / EMOTIONAL / SPIRITUAL
WORK / EDUCATION

DATE OF REVIEW:

MONTH:

CHANGE STARTS WITH A DECISION.

#TrackLife

Monthly Goals

DATE GOALS SET:

LIFESTYLE (E.G. SLEEP, NUTRITION, PUNCTUALITY ETC.)
TECHNICAL / TACTICAL
FAMILY / SOCIAL
PHYSICAL FITNESS / HEALTH
MENTAL / EMOTIONAL / SPIRITUAL
WORK / EDUCATION

Training Overview

WEEKLY TRAINING DIARY

DATE: TRAINING WEEK NO:

MONDAY

TUESDAY

WEDNESDAY

THURSDAY

WEEKLY TRAINING DIARY

FRIDAY

SATURDAY

SUNDAY

NOTES

WEEKLY TRAINING DIARY

DATE: TRAINING WEEK NO:

MONDAY

TUESDAY

WEDNESDAY

THURSDAY

WEEKLY TRAINING DIARY

FRIDAY

SATURDAY

SUNDAY

NOTES

WEEKLY TRAINING DIARY

DATE: TRAINING WEEK NO:

MONDAY

TUESDAY

WEDNESDAY

THURSDAY

WEEKLY TRAINING DIARY

FRIDAY

SATURDAY

SUNDAY

NOTES

WEEKLY TRAINING DIARY

DATE: TRAINING WEEK NO:

MONDAY
TUESDAY
WEDNESDAY
THURSDAY

WEEKLY TRAINING DIARY

FRIDAY

SATURDAY

SUNDAY

NOTES

WEEKLY TRAINING DIARY

DATE: TRAINING WEEK NO:

MONDAY
TUESDAY
WEDNESDAY
THURSDAY

WEEKLY TRAINING DIARY

FRIDAY

SATURDAY

SUNDAY

NOTES

Monthly Goals Review

REVIEW YOUR GOALS FROM THE PAST MONTH.
DID YOU ACHIEVE THEM? IF YES, WHAT WORKED WELL?
IF NOT, WHAT WILL YOU DO DIFFERENTLY NEXT MONTH?

LIFESTYLE (E.G. SLEEP, NUTRITION, PUNCTUALITY ETC.)
TECHNICAL / TACTICAL
FAMILY / SOCIAL
PHYSICAL FITNESS / HEALTH
MENTAL / EMOTIONAL / SPIRITUAL
WORK / EDUCATION

DATE OF REVIEW:

MONTH:

YOU CAN.

#TrackLife

Monthly Goals

DATE GOALS SET:

LIFESTYLE (E.G. SLEEP, NUTRITION, PUNCTUALITY ETC.)
TECHNICAL / TACTICAL
FAMILY / SOCIAL
PHYSICAL FITNESS / HEALTH
MENTAL / EMOTIONAL / SPIRITUAL
WORK / EDUCATION

Training Overview

WEEKLY TRAINING DIARY

DATE: TRAINING WEEK NO:

MONDAY

TUESDAY

WEDNESDAY

THURSDAY

WEEKLY TRAINING DIARY

FRIDAY

SATURDAY

SUNDAY

NOTES

WEEKLY TRAINING DIARY

DATE: TRAINING WEEK NO:

MONDAY

TUESDAY

WEDNESDAY

THURSDAY

WEEKLY TRAINING DIARY

FRIDAY

SATURDAY

SUNDAY

NOTES

WEEKLY TRAINING DIARY

DATE: TRAINING WEEK NO:

MONDAY

TUESDAY

WEDNESDAY

THURSDAY

WEEKLY TRAINING DIARY

FRIDAY

SATURDAY

SUNDAY

NOTES

WEEKLY TRAINING DIARY

DATE: TRAINING WEEK NO:

MONDAY

TUESDAY

WEDNESDAY

THURSDAY

WEEKLY TRAINING DIARY

FRIDAY

SATURDAY

SUNDAY

NOTES

WEEKLY TRAINING DIARY

DATE: TRAINING WEEK NO:

MONDAY

TUESDAY

WEDNESDAY

THURSDAY

WEEKLY TRAINING DIARY

FRIDAY

SATURDAY

SUNDAY

NOTES

Monthly Goals Review

REVIEW YOUR GOALS FROM THE PAST MONTH.
DID YOU ACHIEVE THEM? IF YES, WHAT WORKED WELL?
IF NOT, WHAT WILL YOU DO DIFFERENTLY NEXT MONTH?

LIFESTYLE (E.G. SLEEP, NUTRITION, PUNCTUALITY ETC.)
TECHNICAL / TACTICAL
FAMILY / SOCIAL
PHYSICAL FITNESS / HEALTH
MENTAL / EMOTIONAL / SPIRITUAL
WORK / EDUCATION

DATE OF REVIEW:

MONTH:

ALL THINGS ARE POSSIBLE, BUT YOU MUST FIRST BELIEVE.

Monthly Goals

DATE GOALS SET:

LIFESTYLE (E.G. SLEEP, NUTRITION, PUNCTUALITY ETC.)
TECHNICAL / TACTICAL
FAMILY / SOCIAL
PHYSICAL FITNESS / HEALTH
MENTAL / EMOTIONAL / SPIRITUAL
WORK / EDUCATION

Training Overview

WEEKLY TRAINING DIARY

DATE: TRAINING WEEK NO:

MONDAY

TUESDAY

WEDNESDAY

THURSDAY

WEEKLY TRAINING DIARY

FRIDAY

SATURDAY

SUNDAY

NOTES

WEEKLY TRAINING DIARY

DATE: TRAINING WEEK NO:

MONDAY
TUESDAY
WEDNESDAY
THURSDAY

WEEKLY TRAINING DIARY

FRIDAY

SATURDAY

SUNDAY

NOTES

WEEKLY TRAINING DIARY

DATE: TRAINING WEEK NO:

MONDAY
TUESDAY
WEDNESDAY
THURSDAY

WEEKLY TRAINING DIARY

FRIDAY

SATURDAY

SUNDAY

NOTES

WEEKLY TRAINING DIARY

DATE: TRAINING WEEK NO:

MONDAY

TUESDAY

WEDNESDAY

THURSDAY

WEEKLY TRAINING DIARY

FRIDAY

SATURDAY

SUNDAY

NOTES

WEEKLY TRAINING DIARY

DATE: TRAINING WEEK NO:

MONDAY

TUESDAY

WEDNESDAY

THURSDAY

WEEKLY TRAINING DIARY

FRIDAY

SATURDAY

SUNDAY

NOTES

Monthly Goals Review

REVIEW YOUR GOALS FROM THE PAST MONTH.
DID YOU ACHIEVE THEM? IF YES, WHAT WORKED WELL?
IF NOT, WHAT WILL YOU DO DIFFERENTLY NEXT MONTH?

LIFESTYLE (E.G. SLEEP, NUTRITION, PUNCTUALITY ETC.)
TECHNICAL / TACTICAL
FAMILY / SOCIAL
PHYSICAL FITNESS / HEALTH
MENTAL / EMOTIONAL / SPIRITUAL
WORK / EDUCATION

DATE OF REVIEW:

MONTH:

EMBRACE THE JOURNEY.

#Tracklife

Monthly Goals

DATE GOALS SET:

LIFESTYLE (E.G. SLEEP, NUTRITION, PUNCTUALITY ETC.)
TECHNICAL / TACTICAL
FAMILY / SOCIAL
PHYSICAL FITNESS / HEALTH
MENTAL / EMOTIONAL / SPIRITUAL
WORK / EDUCATION

Training Overview

WEEKLY TRAINING DIARY

DATE: TRAINING WEEK NO:

MONDAY

TUESDAY

WEDNESDAY

THURSDAY

WEEKLY TRAINING DIARY

FRIDAY

SATURDAY

SUNDAY

NOTES

WEEKLY TRAINING DIARY

DATE: TRAINING WEEK NO:

MONDAY

TUESDAY

WEDNESDAY

THURSDAY

WEEKLY TRAINING DIARY

FRIDAY

SATURDAY

SUNDAY

NOTES

WEEKLY TRAINING DIARY

DATE: TRAINING WEEK NO:

MONDAY

TUESDAY

WEDNESDAY

THURSDAY

WEEKLY TRAINING DIARY

FRIDAY

SATURDAY

SUNDAY

NOTES

WEEKLY TRAINING DIARY

DATE: TRAINING WEEK NO:

MONDAY
TUESDAY
WEDNESDAY
THURSDAY

WEEKLY TRAINING DIARY

FRIDAY

SATURDAY

SUNDAY

NOTES

WEEKLY TRAINING DIARY

DATE: TRAINING WEEK NO:

MONDAY

TUESDAY

WEDNESDAY

THURSDAY

WEEKLY TRAINING DIARY

FRIDAY

SATURDAY

SUNDAY

NOTES

Monthly Goals Review

REVIEW YOUR GOALS FROM THE PAST MONTH.
DID YOU ACHIEVE THEM? IF YES, WHAT WORKED WELL?
IF NOT, WHAT WILL YOU DO DIFFERENTLY NEXT MONTH?

LIFESTYLE (E.G. SLEEP, NUTRITION, PUNCTUALITY ETC.)
TECHNICAL / TACTICAL
FAMILY / SOCIAL
PHYSICAL FITNESS / HEALTH
MENTAL / EMOTIONAL / SPIRITUAL
WORK / EDUCATION

DATE OF REVIEW:

MONTH:

DON'T LET DOUBT STEAL YOUR STRENGTH.

Monthly Goals

DATE GOALS SET:

LIFESTYLE (E.G. SLEEP, NUTRITION, PUNCTUALITY ETC.)
TECHNICAL / TACTICAL
FAMILY / SOCIAL
PHYSICAL FITNESS / HEALTH
MENTAL / EMOTIONAL / SPIRITUAL
WORK / EDUCATION

Training Overview

WEEKLY TRAINING DIARY

DATE: TRAINING WEEK NO:

MONDAY

TUESDAY

WEDNESDAY

THURSDAY

WEEKLY TRAINING DIARY

FRIDAY

SATURDAY

SUNDAY

NOTES

WEEKLY TRAINING DIARY

DATE: TRAINING WEEK NO:

MONDAY

TUESDAY

WEDNESDAY

THURSDAY

WEEKLY TRAINING DIARY

FRIDAY

SATURDAY

SUNDAY

NOTES

WEEKLY TRAINING DIARY

DATE:

TRAINING WEEK NO:

MONDAY

TUESDAY

WEDNESDAY

THURSDAY

WEEKLY TRAINING DIARY

FRIDAY

SATURDAY

SUNDAY

NOTES

WEEKLY TRAINING DIARY

DATE: TRAINING WEEK NO:

MONDAY

TUESDAY

WEDNESDAY

THURSDAY

WEEKLY TRAINING DIARY

FRIDAY

SATURDAY

SUNDAY

NOTES

WEEKLY TRAINING DIARY

DATE: TRAINING WEEK NO:

MONDAY
TUESDAY
WEDNESDAY
THURSDAY

WEEKLY TRAINING DIARY

FRIDAY

SATURDAY

SUNDAY

NOTES

Monthly Goals Review

REVIEW YOUR GOALS FROM THE PAST MONTH.
DID YOU ACHIEVE THEM? IF YES, WHAT WORKED WELL?
IF NOT, WHAT WILL YOU DO DIFFERENTLY NEXT MONTH?

LIFESTYLE (E.G. SLEEP, NUTRITION, PUNCTUALITY ETC.)
TECHNICAL / TACTICAL
FAMILY / SOCIAL
PHYSICAL FITNESS / HEALTH
MENTAL / EMOTIONAL / SPIRITUAL
WORK / EDUCATION

DATE OF REVIEW:

MONTH:

IT'S OK TO CHANGE DIRECTIONS, **BUT NEVER GIVE UP!**

Monthly Goals

DATE GOALS SET:

LIFESTYLE (E.G. SLEEP, NUTRITION, PUNCTUALITY ETC.)
TECHNICAL / TACTICAL
FAMILY / SOCIAL
PHYSICAL FITNESS / HEALTH
MENTAL / EMOTIONAL / SPIRITUAL
WORK / EDUCATION

Training Overview

WEEKLY TRAINING DIARY

DATE: TRAINING WEEK NO:

MONDAY
TUESDAY
WEDNESDAY
THURSDAY

WEEKLY TRAINING DIARY

FRIDAY

SATURDAY

SUNDAY

NOTES

WEEKLY TRAINING DIARY

DATE: TRAINING WEEK NO:

MONDAY
TUESDAY
WEDNESDAY
THURSDAY

WEEKLY TRAINING DIARY

FRIDAY

SATURDAY

SUNDAY

NOTES

WEEKLY TRAINING DIARY

DATE: TRAINING WEEK NO:

MONDAY

TUESDAY

WEDNESDAY

THURSDAY

WEEKLY TRAINING DIARY

FRIDAY

SATURDAY

SUNDAY

NOTES

WEEKLY TRAINING DIARY

DATE: TRAINING WEEK NO:

MONDAY

TUESDAY

WEDNESDAY

THURSDAY

WEEKLY TRAINING DIARY

FRIDAY

SATURDAY

SUNDAY

NOTES

WEEKLY TRAINING DIARY

DATE: TRAINING WEEK NO:

MONDAY
TUESDAY
WEDNESDAY
THURSDAY

WEEKLY TRAINING DIARY

FRIDAY

SATURDAY

SUNDAY

NOTES

Monthly Goals Review

REVIEW YOUR GOALS FROM THE PAST MONTH.
DID YOU ACHIEVE THEM? IF YES, WHAT WORKED WELL?
IF NOT, WHAT WILL YOU DO DIFFERENTLY NEXT MONTH?

LIFESTYLE (E.G. SLEEP, NUTRITION, PUNCTUALITY ETC.)
TECHNICAL / TACTICAL
FAMILY / SOCIAL
PHYSICAL FITNESS / HEALTH
MENTAL / EMOTIONAL / SPIRITUAL
WORK / EDUCATION

DATE OF REVIEW:

MONTH:

LIFE CAN BE TOUGH,
SPORT CAN GET ROUGH,
BUT YOU ARE ALWAYS ENOUGH.

Monthly Goals

DATE GOALS SET:

LIFESTYLE (E.G. SLEEP, NUTRITION, PUNCTUALITY ETC.)
TECHNICAL / TACTICAL
FAMILY / SOCIAL
PHYSICAL FITNESS / HEALTH
MENTAL / EMOTIONAL / SPIRITUAL
WORK / EDUCATION

Training Overview

WEEKLY TRAINING DIARY

DATE: TRAINING WEEK NO:

MONDAY
TUESDAY
WEDNESDAY
THURSDAY

WEEKLY TRAINING DIARY

FRIDAY

SATURDAY

SUNDAY

NOTES

WEEKLY TRAINING DIARY

DATE: TRAINING WEEK NO:

MONDAY
TUESDAY
WEDNESDAY
THURSDAY

WEEKLY TRAINING DIARY

FRIDAY

SATURDAY

SUNDAY

NOTES

WEEKLY TRAINING DIARY

DATE: TRAINING WEEK NO:

MONDAY

TUESDAY

WEDNESDAY

THURSDAY

WEEKLY TRAINING DIARY

FRIDAY

SATURDAY

SUNDAY

NOTES

WEEKLY TRAINING DIARY

DATE: TRAINING WEEK NO:

MONDAY

TUESDAY

WEDNESDAY

THURSDAY

WEEKLY TRAINING DIARY

FRIDAY

SATURDAY

SUNDAY

NOTES

WEEKLY TRAINING DIARY

DATE: TRAINING WEEK NO:

MONDAY

TUESDAY

WEDNESDAY

THURSDAY

WEEKLY TRAINING DIARY

FRIDAY

SATURDAY

SUNDAY

NOTES

Monthly Goals Review

REVIEW YOUR GOALS FROM THE PAST MONTH.
DID YOU ACHIEVE THEM? IF YES, WHAT WORKED WELL?
IF NOT, WHAT WILL YOU DO DIFFERENTLY NEXT MONTH?

LIFESTYLE (E.G. SLEEP, NUTRITION, PUNCTUALITY ETC.)
TECHNICAL / TACTICAL
FAMILY / SOCIAL
PHYSICAL FITNESS / HEALTH
MENTAL / EMOTIONAL / SPIRITUAL
WORK / EDUCATION

DATE OF REVIEW:

MONTH:

WHAT YOU CHOOSE TO DO TODAY IS SHAPING YOUR FUTURE...

...WHAT DO YOU CHOOSE?

Tracklife

Monthly Goals

DATE GOALS SET:

LIFESTYLE (E.G. SLEEP, NUTRITION, PUNCTUALITY ETC.)
TECHNICAL / TACTICAL
FAMILY / SOCIAL
PHYSICAL FITNESS / HEALTH
MENTAL / EMOTIONAL / SPIRITUAL
WORK / EDUCATION

Training Overview

WEEKLY TRAINING DIARY

DATE: TRAINING WEEK NO:

MONDAY

TUESDAY

WEDNESDAY

THURSDAY

WEEKLY TRAINING DIARY

FRIDAY

SATURDAY

SUNDAY

NOTES

WEEKLY TRAINING DIARY

DATE:

TRAINING WEEK NO:

MONDAY
TUESDAY
WEDNESDAY
THURSDAY

WEEKLY TRAINING DIARY

FRIDAY

SATURDAY

SUNDAY

NOTES

WEEKLY TRAINING DIARY

DATE: TRAINING WEEK NO:

MONDAY

TUESDAY

WEDNESDAY

THURSDAY

WEEKLY TRAINING DIARY

FRIDAY

SATURDAY

SUNDAY

NOTES

WEEKLY TRAINING DIARY

DATE: TRAINING WEEK NO:

MONDAY

TUESDAY

WEDNESDAY

THURSDAY

WEEKLY TRAINING DIARY

FRIDAY

SATURDAY

SUNDAY

NOTES

WEEKLY TRAINING DIARY

DATE: TRAINING WEEK NO:

MONDAY
TUESDAY
WEDNESDAY
THURSDAY

WEEKLY TRAINING DIARY

FRIDAY
SATURDAY
SUNDAY
NOTES

Monthly Goals Review

REVIEW YOUR GOALS FROM THE PAST MONTH.
DID YOU ACHIEVE THEM? IF YES, WHAT WORKED WELL?
IF NOT, WHAT WILL YOU DO DIFFERENTLY NEXT MONTH?

LIFESTYLE (E.G. SLEEP, NUTRITION, PUNCTUALITY ETC.)
TECHNICAL / TACTICAL
FAMILY / SOCIAL
PHYSICAL FITNESS / HEALTH
MENTAL / EMOTIONAL / SPIRITUAL
WORK / EDUCATION

DATE OF REVIEW:

MONTH:

MANY PEOPLE HAVE DREAMS,
MANY PEOPLE TALK,
BUT ONLY THE BRAVE WALK THE WALK.

Monthly Goals

DATE GOALS SET:

LIFESTYLE (E.G. SLEEP, NUTRITION, PUNCTUALITY ETC.)
TECHNICAL / TACTICAL
FAMILY / SOCIAL
PHYSICAL FITNESS / HEALTH
MENTAL / EMOTIONAL / SPIRITUAL
WORK / EDUCATION

Training Overview

WEEKLY TRAINING DIARY

DATE:

TRAINING WEEK NO:

MONDAY

TUESDAY

WEDNESDAY

THURSDAY

WEEKLY TRAINING DIARY

FRIDAY

SATURDAY

SUNDAY

NOTES

WEEKLY TRAINING DIARY

DATE: TRAINING WEEK NO:

MONDAY

TUESDAY

WEDNESDAY

THURSDAY

WEEKLY TRAINING DIARY

FRIDAY

SATURDAY

SUNDAY

NOTES

WEEKLY TRAINING DIARY

DATE: TRAINING WEEK NO:

MONDAY

TUESDAY

WEDNESDAY

THURSDAY

WEEKLY TRAINING DIARY

FRIDAY

SATURDAY

SUNDAY

NOTES

WEEKLY TRAINING DIARY

DATE: TRAINING WEEK NO:

MONDAY
TUESDAY
WEDNESDAY
THURSDAY

WEEKLY TRAINING DIARY

FRIDAY

SATURDAY

SUNDAY

NOTES

WEEKLY TRAINING DIARY

DATE: TRAINING WEEK NO:

MONDAY
TUESDAY
WEDNESDAY
THURSDAY

WEEKLY TRAINING DIARY

FRIDAY

SATURDAY

SUNDAY

NOTES

Monthly Goals Review

REVIEW YOUR GOALS FROM THE PAST MONTH.
DID YOU ACHIEVE THEM? IF YES, WHAT WORKED WELL?
IF NOT, WHAT WILL YOU DO DIFFERENTLY NEXT MONTH?

LIFESTYLE (E.G. SLEEP, NUTRITION, PUNCTUALITY ETC.)
TECHNICAL / TACTICAL
FAMILY / SOCIAL
PHYSICAL FITNESS / HEALTH
MENTAL / EMOTIONAL / SPIRITUAL
WORK / EDUCATION

DATE OF REVIEW:

MONTH:

THERE'S THE FEAR OF FAILURE,
AND THERE'S THE FEAR OF SUCCESS...

DON'T BE A SLAVE TO EITHER.

Monthly Goals

DATE GOALS SET:

LIFESTYLE (E.G. SLEEP, NUTRITION, PUNCTUALITY ETC.)
TECHNICAL / TACTICAL
FAMILY / SOCIAL
PHYSICAL FITNESS / HEALTH
MENTAL / EMOTIONAL / SPIRITUAL
WORK / EDUCATION

Training Overview

WEEKLY TRAINING DIARY

DATE: TRAINING WEEK NO:

MONDAY
TUESDAY
WEDNESDAY
THURSDAY

WEEKLY TRAINING DIARY

FRIDAY

SATURDAY

SUNDAY

NOTES

WEEKLY TRAINING DIARY

DATE: TRAINING WEEK NO:

MONDAY
TUESDAY
WEDNESDAY
THURSDAY

WEEKLY TRAINING DIARY

FRIDAY

SATURDAY

SUNDAY

NOTES

WEEKLY TRAINING DIARY

DATE: TRAINING WEEK NO:

MONDAY
TUESDAY
WEDNESDAY
THURSDAY

WEEKLY TRAINING DIARY

FRIDAY

SATURDAY

SUNDAY

NOTES

WEEKLY TRAINING DIARY

DATE: TRAINING WEEK NO:

MONDAY
TUESDAY
WEDNESDAY
THURSDAY

WEEKLY TRAINING DIARY

FRIDAY

SATURDAY

SUNDAY

NOTES

WEEKLY TRAINING DIARY

DATE: TRAINING WEEK NO:

MONDAY

TUESDAY

WEDNESDAY

THURSDAY

WEEKLY TRAINING DIARY

FRIDAY

SATURDAY

SUNDAY

NOTES

Monthly Goals Review

REVIEW YOUR GOALS FROM THE PAST MONTH.
DID YOU ACHIEVE THEM? IF YES, WHAT WORKED WELL?
IF NOT, WHAT WILL YOU DO DIFFERENTLY NEXT MONTH?

LIFESTYLE (E.G. SLEEP, NUTRITION, PUNCTUALITY ETC.)
TECHNICAL / TACTICAL
FAMILY / SOCIAL
PHYSICAL FITNESS / HEALTH
MENTAL / EMOTIONAL / SPIRITUAL
WORK / EDUCATION

DATE OF REVIEW:

MONTH:

SUCCESS IS NOT DEFINED BY WINNING OR LOSING ...

...*PAUSE AND THINK ON THAT!*

Monthly Goals

DATE GOALS SET:

LIFESTYLE (E.G. SLEEP, NUTRITION, PUNCTUALITY ETC.)
TECHNICAL / TACTICAL
FAMILY / SOCIAL
PHYSICAL FITNESS / HEALTH
MENTAL / EMOTIONAL / SPIRITUAL
WORK / EDUCATION

Training Overview

WEEKLY TRAINING DIARY

DATE: TRAINING WEEK NO:

MONDAY

TUESDAY

WEDNESDAY

THURSDAY

WEEKLY TRAINING DIARY

FRIDAY

SATURDAY

SUNDAY

NOTES

WEEKLY TRAINING DIARY

DATE: TRAINING WEEK NO:

MONDAY
TUESDAY
WEDNESDAY
THURSDAY

WEEKLY TRAINING DIARY

FRIDAY

SATURDAY

SUNDAY

NOTES

WEEKLY TRAINING DIARY

DATE: TRAINING WEEK NO:

MONDAY
TUESDAY
WEDNESDAY
THURSDAY

WEEKLY TRAINING DIARY

FRIDAY

SATURDAY

SUNDAY

NOTES

WEEKLY TRAINING DIARY

DATE: TRAINING WEEK NO:

MONDAY
TUESDAY
WEDNESDAY
THURSDAY

WEEKLY TRAINING DIARY

FRIDAY

SATURDAY

SUNDAY

NOTES

WEEKLY TRAINING DIARY

DATE: TRAINING WEEK NO:

MONDAY

TUESDAY

WEDNESDAY

THURSDAY

WEEKLY TRAINING DIARY

FRIDAY

SATURDAY

SUNDAY

NOTES

Monthly Goals Review

REVIEW YOUR GOALS FROM THE PAST MONTH.
DID YOU ACHIEVE THEM? IF YES, WHAT WORKED WELL?
IF NOT, WHAT WILL YOU DO DIFFERENTLY NEXT MONTH?

LIFESTYLE (E.G. SLEEP, NUTRITION, PUNCTUALITY ETC.)
TECHNICAL / TACTICAL
FAMILY / SOCIAL
PHYSICAL FITNESS / HEALTH
MENTAL / EMOTIONAL / SPIRITUAL
WORK / EDUCATION

DATE OF REVIEW:

End Of Season Review

MY TOP 5 PERFORMANCES THIS SEASON

HIGHLIGHTS & POSITIVES FROM THIS SEASON

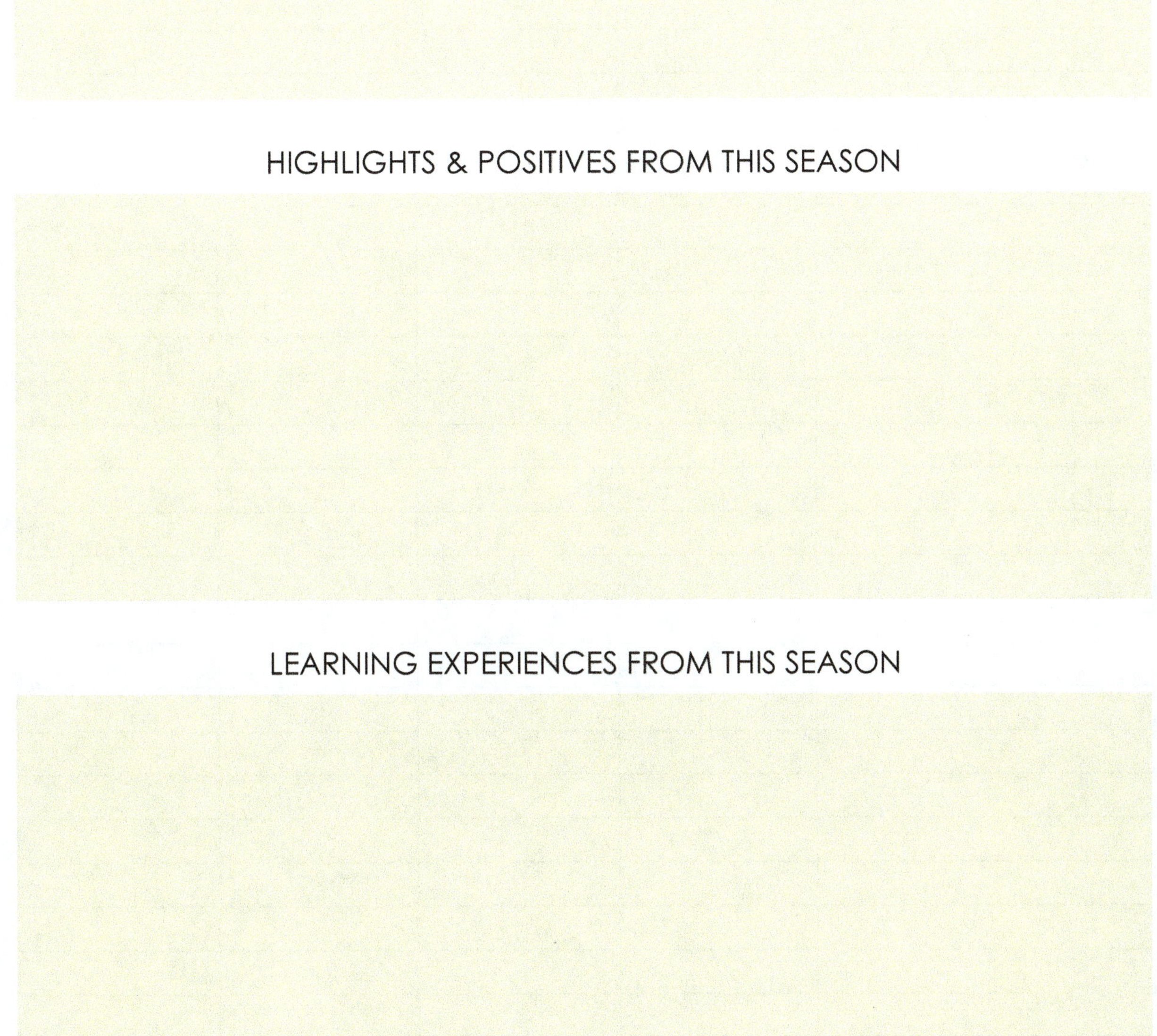

LEARNING EXPERIENCES FROM THIS SEASON

Training Records

Exercise / Distance	Date	PB / PR	Date	PB / PR
E.g., Back squat	01.05.23	110kg	01.08.23	130kg
E.g., 10m from blocks	02.01.23	1.94s	02.04.23	1.86s

NOTES

NOTES

NOTES

www.ingramcontent.com/pod-product-compliance
Lightning Source LLC
Chambersburg PA
CBHW080913190726
48294CB00009B/2071
9781838436872